Let's Read the
Christmas Story

For Lucie A.A.

Text by Lois Rock
Illustrations copyright © 1999 Alex Ayliffe
This edition copyright © 2004 Lion Hudson

The moral rights of the author and illustrator
have been asserted

A Lion Children's Book
an imprint of
Lion Hudson plc
Mayfield House, 256 Banbury Road,
Oxford OX2 7DH, England
www.lionhudson.com
ISBN 0 7459 4904 5

First edition 2004
1 3 5 7 9 10 8 6 4 2

Typeset in 32/46 Kidprint MT Bold
Printed and bound in Singapore

**This Bible tale is adapted from the story of Jesus' birth,
which can be found in Matthew, chapters 1–2, and Luke, chapter 2**

let's read the
Christmas Story

Retold by Lois Rock ✷ Illustrated by Alex Ayliffe

LION
CHILDREN'S

Mary goes with Joseph

down to Bethlehem.

A crowded inn,

a stable room:

an ox makes room for them.

The baby Jesus,
swaddling bands:

but oh! – no baby bed.

Some hay, a blanket:

in a manger,

Jesus rests his head.

A flock of sheep

and shepherds, who watch
them through the night.

An angel with a message...

more angels shining bright.

The shepherds
go to Bethlehem,

just as the angels say.

They find the baby Jesus,

still sleeping in the hay.

The night-time sky:

some wise men
are following a star.

It lights the road to Bethlehem

where Mary and Jesus are.

Gold, frankincense,

a box of myrrh:

these are gifts they bring

for little baby Jesus
of whom the angels sing.

Other titles in this series from
Lion Children's Books

let's read the
Noah's Ark Story

0 7459 4905 3

let's read the
Lost Sheep Story

0 7459 4932 0